T0149314

Good-Bye POEMS

Humorous and Serious Thoughts

ALBERT MORGAN

WESTBOW
PRESS®
A DIVISION OF THOMAS NELSON
& ZONDERVAN

WestBow Press books may be ordered through booksellers or by contacting:

WestBow Press
A Division of Thomas Nelson & Zondervan
1663 Liberty Drive
Bloomington, IN 47403
www.westbowpress.com
1 (866) 928-1240

ISBN: 978-1-5127-7615-7 (sc)
ISBN: 978-1-5127-7616-4 (e)

Library of Congress Control Number: 2017902579

Print information available on the last page.

WestBow Press rev. date: 03/19/2019

Table of Contents

Introduction

The purpose of this poetry is dual. Firstly, for humor and entertainment so we can appreciate the things we have. Secondly, to get people to think of the very serious and sobering times we are living in.

In life, we all experience things that break down or wear away and need to be replaced or repaired. We can take clothes or items for granted. When certain things are worn away or no longer function, we are forced to take notice. A malfunctioning hot-water tank, for example, will really be missed. Like many a property owner, the author knows about the frustration and expenses to replace things. He puts a humorous spin on things with rhymes.

For example: "Good-Bye, faithful underwear, I will always remember us as a happy pair.

But there is no doubt you are all worn out. You have lost your elasticity; therefore, I will have to

dispose of you as fast as electricity."

"Good-Bye, suppository. You are important, but you get no glory."

"Good-Bye, toilet bowl. I must rid you; that is my goal."

"Good-Bye, toothbrush; have to get rid of you in a rush."

"Good-Bye, longtime refrigerator. I cannot say, 'See you later.'"

In *Poor Richard's Almanac*, Benjamin Franklin stated, "When the well's dry, we know the

worth of water." We can appreciate big or small conveniences in life.

From a religious and serious perspective: "Good-Bye, America. Sorry to see you go, seeing your character and morals have sunk so low."

"Even So, Come, Lord Jesus" is a prophetic poem. "Good-Bye, Death and Grave" speaks of things and life being temporary. The author ends certain poems with a biblical prophetic and positive message:

there is a future hope beyond our physical existence.

To Gisela, my poem pen pal, and to friends who encouraged and helped me to share these poems with others.

A Big Relief

I went to a dance one night organized by Eric.

Upon arrival, I suddenly became hysteric,

for I saw my big sister, Gisela,

who liked and ate too much mozzarella.

When I saw how much she had spread,

I said to myself, "O dread!"

It would have been better dancing with a bear

than with my bloated, gargantuan friend right there.

After lifting her, I couldn't stand up straight

because she had put on all of that weight.

So bent was I and out of shape,

I could only walk like an ape.

Never did I realize I could be so blue

because there was no solution, not even a clue.

When I came out of the dream, it was a big relief,

a feeling so good and beyond belief.

At a future dance with Gisela,

we can dance to a lively tarantella.

I never thought that this lively miss

would one day become my delightful "big sis."

I can always look back and say I was a fortunate fella

to have met and enjoyed the dances with Gisela.

My Sorella (sister)

It is good to think of Gisela

as my wonderful and big sorella.

When we dance together on the floor,

its time well spent and never a bore,

for we move together with our feet,

and enjoy ourselves as we stay with the beat.

Since our thinking is youthful and enthusiastic,

we don't mind being a little gymnastic.

When she slides or is hoisted in the air,

she doesn't worry-enjoys-how very rare!

How can one find someone of this sort,

full of enthusiasm and such a good sport?

It's fine to dance with her to a waltz,

thinking of her as genuine-not someone false.

What we hope that will never become passe',

is the lively rhythm of the merengue.

By dipping and wrapping we put on a good show,

stirring and turning to the elegant tango.

As two innocent children busy at play,

we do our best with the paso doble.

The hustle, salsa, samba, and swing,

tell us truly that this is our thing.

At the sound of the quick-step and two-step,

it's fortunate that we have the energy and pep.

The fox-trot, rhumba, and cha cha music we hear,

keeps us dancing around with much good cheer.

We may finish with a polka at the end of the night,

whirling and hopping with all of our might.

It is good that Gisela was never a nun;

otherwise, how could we have so much fun?

Her company and friendship are certainly a pleasure,

something in this world that exceeds fame and great treasure.

She may think when we dance I'm a little crazy,

but that's all right; she knows I'm not lazy,

for we do work and move, and dance hard;

it's good for the health and keeps off the lard.

We can always hold on to the thoughts of good times,

and, perhaps, better remember them by the use of these rhymes.

At this time we may be far away, but

there is hope to be together on another day,

so that I can be with Gisela,

my wonderful and big sorella.

Good-Bye, Single Life

My darling sweet potato,

do you carrot for me?

With your radish hair and turnip nose,

you are the apple of my eye.

When I think of you, I sigh.

By staring at me with your large, dark grape like eyes that bulge,

there is so much that you divulge.

Though you may not be lean

as a string bean,

and have hips of large watermelon size,

I still think you are a great prize.

If we cantaloupe, lettuce get married;

I am sure we would make a happy pear;

don't you think that would be good and fair?

A wedding date

would be something to celerybrate.

The spinach I cook would keep us going strong;

how could we go wrong?

So what if you don't sing well or dance?

You are like the delectable eggplants.

It is happiness for me when we meet;

you are something hard to beet.

They say I am desperate and you really have a big nose;

regardless, to me you have a great pose.

I didn't know where you came from;

at first sight I saw you as a plum.

During time at the beach,

you remind me of a round peach.

I ignore your bunions,

and think of sweet onions.

I don't care if they call you a lemon;

you're like a gift from heaven.

When you gracefully give your hair a stroke,

you remind me of a beautiful artichoke.

Even though your teeth may be a little crooked and number just few,

you, to me, are like those luscious melons we call, "honeydew".

As a queen to me, you make me think of a broccoli crown;

there is no way I could give you a frown.

I always want to be with you till death,

even in spite of your garlic breath.

Your skin may not be all wrinkle free,

but you are like a cup of strawberries to me.

With your fineries on and after a shower,

you have that freshness of a cauliflower.

You are a sweet tangerine,

one who is never mean.

To the beaches would I take you to swim and wash;

you would come out looking clean as a cucumber and squash.

Your enormous flat feet are so appealing and fine;

you can stomp on the grapes to make my wine.

With your shoulders so wide and great,

you could support and carry an orange crate.

As the grapefruit,

for you I root.

The long lobes that came with you when born

make me think of appealing ears of freshly picked corn.

Don't worry if you're a little stooped in the back;

who would notice when you carry a potato sack?

Even if you can cook only escarole, beans and rice,

to me your are someone of great price.

Your loving peddler

Good-Bye, Waist Tire

If this applies to you, say good-bye to your waist tire;

diet, exercise, and don't be afraid to perspire.

This is one tire you want to lose;

this is the way to choose.

So here is the tip that is sound;

you don't have to be so round.

By carrying around that waist tire,

it's not something you need and desire.

It's hard to hide a waist tire,

even when covered with baggy attire.

If your arms and legs resemble wheels,

rid the sweets, work out, and see how good it feels.

Here is a way you can become a successful loser:

eat the vegetables and salads; become a mover.

You do not have to have your waist tire on display;

there is hope; you can make it go away.

The waist tire is not something you have to wear;

work out, get active in the good fresh air.

Stay with natural foods; study good nutrition;

this would be a great ambition.

Throw away the cigarette, dope, and weed.

These are the things you don't need.

Don't say, "There is no hope";

be positive; don't think like a dope.

You don't have to be in the waist tire rut;

get going; you can get rid of the gut.

Don't put it off and wait;

you'll look better and feel great.

So, for a healthier you,

get moving and these things do.

Free yourself from the bulging waist line:

improve your physical condition and design.

No need to have people noticing you with their eyes

and thinking to themselves, *Thunder thighs.*

Don't sit down and become passive and quiet.

I repeat: exercise and learn the right diet.

Prove something and give yourself that chance;

the only price will be buying smaller dresses and pants.

But that is a price that is small;

your life quality will be better after all.

You don't have to be called a fat slob;

be like the diligent athlete training for the job.

Never overdo or strain;

the idea is to train.

Think young and thin;

keep that discipline within.

With determination and work, watch the fat melt:

you will be delighted as you keep tightening the belt.

There's no need to agonize

by the thought of exercise.

In my seventy-first year, one-hand push-ups I still can do.

From a geezer: think, younger people, the potentials for you.

(By the way, young geezer.)

I can still kick over my head.

Say not to yourself, "Exercise? Oh, dread!"

I hope my words to you are encouraging and ample

so that I can be, at least to some, a good example.

Good-Bye, Tire

Good-bye, tire.

Your service time has to expire.

The invention of the wheel or tire

is that old idea we still can admire.

With your shape so round,

people can cover so much ground.

Once you were a great wheel,

but you have to go for real.

As you rolled over many a thing,

in the car I could hum or sing.

I bought you secondhand.

You carried me over much land.

You looked good to me when you were sold,

but now you are getting bald and old.

Your threads are worn and hardly show;

you won't make it through the ice or snow.

Who wants to worry and perspire

over such a worn tire?

I have to do something I do not desire;

now I have to buy another tire.

With the hole in your side, you became flat;

I wanted to hold on to you, but I can't keep you like that.

Seeing that you are beyond repair,

I can say you served well and did your share.

Good-Bye, Hot Water Tank

Good-bye, hot water tank.

When I saw your condition, my heart sank.

You no longer hold water; you got weak.

I see so much water leak.

It certainly is an eyesore

to see so much water cover the floor.

Again, I have to call the plumber;

you had to break down when it's no longer summer.

You wore out and got old;

now the water comes out cold.

Since you are no longer so hot,

I have to remove you from your spot.

No one could be thrilled

showering in water so chilled.

The floor is quite wet;

you give me another debt.

Having you in the house was once a delight;

I could shower well, day or night.

We can be thankful for a tank that provides a hot shower

that we can enjoy at any hour.

So, tank, since you cannot supply hot water,

a new tank I will now order.

The warm water it will provide

will be a welcomed feeling for my hide.

Now I have a new hot water thing

and am content for the warmth it does bring.

I look forward to getting in the shower

and once again sing with power.

The Bible says, "In everything give thanks (1 Thess. 5:18);

at this time, I can be more thankful for hot water tanks.

No longer do I look at the shower and stall;

I just go in and get plenty of hot water after all.

Spiritual analogy: don't stop doing works that are Godly and good;

Revelation 2:5 makes that plain and easy to be understood.

Unlike that once efficient, reliable hot water tank,

we don't want to quit and at judgment appear unprofitable, cold, and blank.

Good-Bye, Refrigerator

Good-bye, longtime refrigerator.

I cannot say, "See you later."

It's too bad you have to go;

at one time, you had much food to show.

You provided me with such wonderful service.

With your weight and size, disposing of you makes me nervous.

As long as a refrigerator's motor can well run,

you and people can be like one.

Refrigerators in a house

sometimes attract more interest than a spouse.

The refrigerator is a wonderful thing to assemble.

Unfortunately, as people eat, like you they resemble.

You held the wine and the beer

to help people be of good cheer.

Your function was to preserve the food

so people can eat and be in a good mood.

For some reason, you no longer turn water into ice;

on a hot day, for me, that wasn't very nice.

Another thing you have lacking:

the plastic in you falls and is cracking.

I tried to hold on and save you with duct tape;

unfortunately, for you, there is no escape.

The door doesn't close and firmly stay,

another reason to move you away.

I tried hard to keep you, be frugal, and economize,

but to keep you just isn't wise.

Your inner lining of rubber keeps falling;

that, to me, is appalling.

You no longer keep the food cold.

I must move you; for me, that is bold.

I can be a miser for so long,

but to keep you would be wrong.

Like Mr. Jack Benny,

I try to watch every penny.

Realizing I have to replace you with another, my heart sank;

with sadness, I haul you out and break the bank.

PS: On a positive note, I can say, of you, I got my money's worth

while I was alive on this earth.

Good-Bye, Old Shoe

Good-bye, old shoe.

I remember when you were new.

You were with me for many a decade,

but you're worn and away you fade.

You know, shoe,

a good service is what you do.

Our feet are too sensitive, shoe,

for the tasks and things you go through.

Your tough, cool leather

protects us in all kinds of weather,

from hard, sharp things in the dirt,

which could, otherwise, cause our feet to hurt.

Cannot say how many miles with me you walked;

but unlike people, you never squawked.

You had a wonderful sole and heel,

at a good cost and deal.

Even with trips to the repair shop,

a shoe's life comes to a stop.

When I think and look at you, shoe,

in a sense, part of us, our feet, live in you.

Unlike the stressed lady with many kids living in a shoe,

at least I know what to do; your time to retire is due.

I remember with you I could walk and run;

thanks for the service, shoe, for a mission well done.

Here is a thought I could share:

be thankful for shoes that give good foot care.

So off to the shoe store I go;

thought I, *A good way to spend the dough.*

Even if money in our life is only a little bit,

we can be thankful for a shoe of a good fit.

Good-Bye, Car

Good-bye, but sorry to see you go, car;
you've taken me places near and far.
One time you were an impressive hunk;
now I have to send you to the junk.
You're leaking all this oil,
getting it on pavement and soil.
Your age makes it hard to find a certain part;
sometimes you shut off on me and refuse to start.
I held on to you for many a year;
to me, you were that dear.
When you had transmission trouble,
I got you repaired on the double.
When none of your windows would open or close,
to the occasion I rose.
Spending so much on repairs for a car to work
can sometimes make one feel like a jerk.
When you were reliable and could well run,
you carried me to work or places for good times and fun.
Twenty-one years old are you;
how much money on you I blew.
Many times I drove you along,
wondering what else could go wrong.

Thanks for carrying me and cargo for many a mile;

that's why I hung on to you for a long while.

The day you are towed away will make me sad,

but at least I know you were not all that bad.

Good-Bye, Faithful Underwear

Good-bye, my faithful underwear.

I will always remember us as a happy pair.

But there is no doubt

that you are all worn out.

You have lost your elasticity;

therefore, I will have to dispose of you as

fast as electricity.

As time went on, you became old,

since the day to me you were sold.

Even though you can no longer hold up and

yourself support,

I will always consider you to be a good sport.

Though you have been many times through the washing machine,

you always came out looking good and never mean

you always came out from the dryer;

you were something I needed and could always admire.

After a wash, you never much shrunk

or even stunk.

You clung to me faithfully during many a dance

and got no recognition being hidden under the pants.

I didn't have to check on you either, not even a glance,

for I knew you were always there.

So good-bye, my faithful underwear.

You were with me everywhere,

whether walking or sitting in a chair.

Unfortunately, you are something I have to dispose;

in life, that's the way it goes.

Even though you have the status of Fruit of the Loom,

in my drawer for you is no longer any room.

You had to put up with a lot of perspiration,

but underwear gets no recognition or adoration.

If some unfortunate soul is afflicted with diarrhea,

you become a vulnerable target at any time of the year.

There should be a national holiday for the lowly,

thankless position of underwear, which merits no pay;

they are just here for a while and then tossed away.

There should be cookouts, and we should not be afraid

to have a great underwear parade.

Of this garment, we should become aware by making underwear-like

flags and various styles and colors to give it some dignity,

for the young and old to see how they can be made so pretty.

A paid national underwear holiday should be mandatory

to give this taken-for-granted garment some dignity and glory.

After all, the underwear is always dear,

faithfully covering the derriere.

We should be more aware of the glorious underwear

and, with awesome respect to it, stare.

Good-bye, again, my underwear; you were the faithful,

accommodating friend

who for me would bend to the very end.

PS.

Another thought came to me, underwear, so dear.

I could start you out on a new career;

even though on me you fall and sag,

maybe I could use you as a dust rag.

To me it is an idea that is so nifty

since I am so frugal and thrifty.

Good-Bye, Faucet and Sink

Good-bye, old faucet;

Looking at you, I say, "Time to toss it."

I tried so hard to seek

a way to stop the water leak.

Water continues to drip;

on and on the drops slip.

Wasted water goes down the drain;

you got to be a bit of a pain.

And you, bathroom sink,

make me think:

you are peeling and losing your paint;

new is something you just ain't.

I see the cracks in you and lines,

more of the aging signs.

For forty years you stayed,

but you lasted long for what I paid.

I have to replace you;

I guess that is something overdue.

Now I have to call for the plumber;

more expense, another bummer.

Faucet and sink, you may not be again seen,

but I'm thankful you helped keep things and hands clean.

A thought for others, and myself, I remind:

in this world, for some, good water is hard to find.

We can take for granted the luxury of the faucet and sink;

thankfully, we can wash, clean, and easily get a drink.

Good-bye, Screw

I cannot keep you lying around, screw;
there is an important task for you to do.
As I looked and searched around,
I'm glad it is you I found.
Sometimes the screw can be a little prize,
especially when you need one of the right size.
This little item can be used for so much good
to hold together the metal and the wood.
Often unnoticed is the screw
but so important like the glue.
So, screw, get ready;
you have to hold something steady.
Little things can be important, as we know;
I have a place for you to go.
The screw may seem so small
but has a purpose after all.
You may not be large, screw,
but what would we do without you?
A day came when I had to be a "screwup", rightfully called,
using screws for ceiling sheet rock that I installed.
We can take a lesson from the screw in a certain way;
a kind word, call a good deed can make someone's day.

People may think they don't count or matter; they may feel small;

by serving we can make the difference in a life after all.

Mother said, "I sometimes feel like the screw in a chair or table;"

the unnoticed screw is what keeps things together and stable.

To me, this good attitude of support

demonstrates an attitude of a good sport.

As a number of screws hold together the metal and the wood,

so a team of people working together can do so much good.

From the little lone screw, there can be something to learn;

only one person may see a need for someone and show concern.

Good-bye, screw; since you will be out of sight,

I trust you will hold this item of mine tight.

So now that I have you,

do a good job as you pass through.

Thanks again; you're popular, screw;

stores carry many like you.

Now I have you placed; you will be fine there;

you may be small, yet such important hardware.

To the reader I would like to reiterate;

do not of yourself underestimate.

As the screw holds and supports metal and wood,

one person can support, fill in and accomplish good.

Not all are called to nobility, or to perform a great thing;

but by serving in a small way, we never know what good we bring.

By being faithful, honest and dependable with matters small,

potentially, we could be doing greater things after all. Luke 16:10

Good-Bye, Hair

Good-bye, hair.
Sorry to see you are no longer
there.
When you were with me, how
good it was;
now you left me without
even a fuzz.
I had such a good crop;
you left me with nothing on top.
On my head, one time, you were
so thick; now you abandoned me and left
me bald slick.
Years ago, you showed so
many curls;
they helped me to be popular
with the girls.
You displayed many a wave,
but I couldn't hold on to you
and save.
Gradually, you left me one by one;
a strand, you left me none.
On me you were like a frame,
but now I am not the same.

Good-Bye, Hair

I thought, if one has a bald
head that gives a shine,
at least be thankful if your
health is fine.
There is a positive idea I
have this day;
I will get a wig or a fine-looking toupee.
People spend so much on care
for appearance of their hair.
I remind myself that life isn't
all about hair care
but truthfulness and being fair.
A thing to remember: it is not
what is on top of the head
but honestly, kindness, and good
character beneath that count instead.

Good-Bye, Ice Skates

Hate to say this, but good-bye, ice skates;
you were good companions, even better than some dates.
Your boots cannot give me the support
that I need to continue the skating sport.
For years you held up well;
the skating was so invigorating and swell.
Since you are starting to corrode,
it's another reason for you to hit the road.
You were smooth and new;
the skating sport on me grew.
You gave me a mental and physical challenge to be on ice
learning to execute athletic moves and be precise.
It's surprising how one can learn to spin
with precision on your blades so thin.
You were able to help me to stay fit
and not be a couch potato and just sit.
When the skater moves fast or slows,
mentally or physically, one has to be on toes.
One skating champion called skating the loneliest sport,
but that is for an individual of a particular sort.
With your fine boots and shining blades of steel,
being on the ice with you was an exhilarating feel.

You helped me to learn discipline and drive,

even in spite of falls or an unexpected dive.

You served me well, ice skates;

we were something like soul mates.

You were with me for many a session and skate day,

but your steel from sharpening is wearing away.

Now I have to get another pair

because of all your wear.

Cheapskates? You were not cheap;

for me your price was kind of steep.

Skates, even if you have to go and are old,

there is a lesson and thought of you I can hold:

in freestyle skating, it's never a thrill

to fall and take a spill.

There is this thought that comes to mind:

the wise saying of Proverbs 24:16 one can find.

The proverb speaks of falling or failure but a time to rise;

this is good encouragement for those who wish to be wise.

As in skating, life can have setbacks, mistakes, and many a fall,

but we must get up and keep going; a good lesson for us all.

Good-Bye, Mattress

Good-bye, mattress, since you continue to sag;
the discomfort you cause on my back continues to nag.
One-third of my days were spent sleeping on you;
in those hours, we were together like glue.
You were comfortable, even if I could not sleep;
I may have been in thoughts so deep.
Everyone needs a comfortable rest,
but, mattress, you're no longer at your best.
Your springs are sticking out and digging in my back;
it's getting to be a problem when I hit the sack.
To be frugal, I flipped you over on your other side,
but another spring was jabbing my hide.
Turning you over, I thought, might make you last,
but you are now just a thing of the past.
For a comfortable sleep, I would like to be assured;
I tried to hang on to you, but only so much can be endured.
I have to say that one time you were great;
for years you supported all of my weight.
Now that you have sunk so low,
you're another item that has to go.
To the mattress store I go with dread,
forced to spend more to replace you for my bed.

Good-Bye, Roof Shingles

Good-bye, shingles, on this roof of mine;

unfortunately, you're not doing so fine.

You cannot stop the rain;

repairs are in vain.

You always appear looking right,

since you were well placed and on tight.

A protective coating did no good;

the water keeps coming through the wood.

When the rain comes night or day,

I have to move the bed out of the way.

Pans have to be placed on the flooring

when the rain starts pouring.

The water goes through the ceiling;

oh, what a terrible feeling.

If you could only speak,

but no one can find the leak.

To have water dropping on a sleeper's head

is definitely a situation to dread.

Shingles, you just have to go;

you don't stop the rain or snow.

Now I spent money on new shingles,

my pockets are empty; money no longer jingles.

Now, as the rain pours down,

I can sleep and not worry if I drown.

At least I have a good roof over my head

and can sleep on a dry, waterproof, comfortable bed.

Good-Bye, Sneakers

I have to say good-bye to you, each sneaker,

because you are worn out and are weaker.

You are full of holes

from toe to soles.

You took a lot of abuse

from so much use.

I didn't regret owning you a bit

because you helped me to stay physically fit.

Gone is much of your rubber,

but running on you kept off the blubber.

In basketball, I could run and hop,

but you're so worn from bottom to top.

I tried to keep you looking clean

by placing you in the washing machine.

So with regret I throw you in the trash;

to replace you, I have to come up with the cash.

We can appreciate the sneakers for being pliable;

they are much needed, comfortable, and reliable.

Whether you are tall or short,

sneakers are good for wearing or engaging in sport.

Good-Bye, Sock

Good-bye to you, sock,

but I have to drop you like a rock.

How long with me you have been,

but you've worn out so thin.

What you now expose

are more of my toes.

You hang down and got a little floppy,

making me look a bit sloppy.

I can even see some of my heel.

Can't keep you; that's how I feel.

I'm thankful that through rain or sleet,

you helped to warm my feet.

Socks take a lot of pressure and get crushed

as people stand or run when they are rushed.

For you, I can do only so much sewing,

but I guess you have to get going.

It's a good thing you have no sense of smell;

it would be a life for you not so swell.

Good-bye again, lowly sock,

for service and comfort around the clock.

Next time I go to the Dollar Store,

I will break down and buy one pair more.

Good-Bye, Suppository

Good-Bye, suppository,
you are important but get no glory.
No one would want to follow you where you go,
yet you're expected to get results and put on a good show.
You were never meant to be in the limelight, out in the front,
but as some forgotten people, placed at the end; you are only a runt.
You get no thanks for people you must unclog,
even though they stuff themselves like a hog.
Some get constipated and don't know how;
to the rescue you come, and for little you, they may bow.
We all have to be of the belief
your purpose is to bring relief.
You go where there is no shiny sun;
for you or the afflicted, it is not a time for fun.
Jokingly, you have been called in Italian, innuendo;
that is the place you are destined to go.
You may never be remembered or seen again, but
for people you do a good deed;
for you there is a definite need.
Like some people, you may seem insignificant and small;
remember, you can be important; like people, there is a place
for you after all.

Good-Bye, Toilet Bowl

Good-bye, toilet bowl.

I must rid you; that is my goal.

Your inner mechanisms no longer function;

I must throw you out with no compunction.

At one time, being in a rush,

I gave you a flush.

Instead of doing your job,

you almost made me sob.

You overflowed and flooded the floor,

an experience I had to abhor.

I appreciate your service of the past;

now I have to get rid of you, fast.

At one time, you were looking so fine;

you even had a nice shine.

As a stately chair,

you looked so fair.

I have to say that toilets are more important to own

and needed more than a king's throne.

Drunks come to them crawling,

so sick they appear bawling.

People make use of them every day;

toilets complain not and receive no pay.

They provide a unique, smooth seat,
well designed and hard to beat.
I will try not to be too uncouth,
but you have lost your newness like youth.
Thanks again, toilet bowl, for a good show;
for you it is "adios" and time to go.
What you had to put up with and see
is something far beyond me.
I didn't envy your life for what you would take;
for people, it would be a heartache.

Good-Bye, Toilet Paper

Good-Bye, toilet paper, for real;

you are only a one-time deal.

You are something so needed and reliable;

I cannot think of another service, which you

provide, more undesirable.

After people put you to use,

you end up with so much abuse.

When new in the stores, you are white, clean,

and packaged so brightly;

when people are finished with you,

you appear so unsightly.

People blow their noses on you;

suddenly you are tossed and all through.

Many things are you used for to clean and wipe;

yet, from you, not even a gripe.

It is good that you are soft and not rough;

that is why, for people, you are such good stuff.

Precious are you with every sheet

as you faithfully hang by the toilet seat.

Computers and gadgets are things that are adored;

the lowly toilet paper is forgotten and ignored.

It would be a bad day

if toilet paper were taken away.

You are not very strong;

it is good that your life is not long.

Again, toilet paper, so long;

we know, with us, you always belong.

Good-Bye, Toothbrush

Sorry to say this but good-bye, toothbrush;

have to get rid of you in a rush.

You are so worn away,

I cannot have you stay.

Your bristles fall out one by one.

Some get in my mouth; that's no fun.

Whether a toothbrush is north or south,

it's always placed in someone's mouth.

You were put to a good use and not to waste

as you dutifully held the toothpaste.

I appreciate your long service

to help us stay away from dentists, making one nervous.

The toothbrush keeps our teeth looking clean and bright

so we can all be a pleasing and presentable sight.

Thanks again, toothbrush, for helping to fight tooth decay

and to keep all those unwanted cavities away.

Bible, You Are Incredible

Bible, you have an incredible history
of being to most a great mystery.
People find you hard to understand and believe;
many have tried but cannot perceive.
Copies of you are on shelves for display,
but little attention to you people pay.
For the lives of some, you are a must;
for others, you are placed to collect dust.
Of you, most people know little about.
What you say cause many to doubt.
During an oath, people place their hands on you to swear,
but what is printed in you they do not care.
Many consider you irrelevant in life;
by ignoring you, the world suffers with strife.
Some think they are upright and swell;
just one show of truth from you, watch them rebel.
People do not want to hear what you quote;
they reject what the Almighty inspired and wrote.

To mention the name of Jesus or God in a public place
could possibly bring about derision and disgrace.
To put you out of existence, men have made an attempt.

Contrary are you to their ways; they hold you in contempt.

Copies of you have been burned,

an example of how you are spurned.

Some delighted in your truths, which they cherished;

for you they faced martyrdom and perished.

The world finds you abrasive,

hides from you and is evasive.

It rejects your correction,

resulting in no righteous direction.

You show purpose, way to life eternal, how to be wise;

unfortunately, you are a book that many despise.

In business, you are merchandise for top sales;

to follow what you stand for, humanity fails.

For an educator to say your words are divinely inspired

may disqualify him for a position or even be fired.

One teacher who gave a student a copy of you

was discharged and his job all through.

We see what you are preaching

goes against scientific teaching.

You speak of a creator; to many this takes nerve

to take credit and attention you do not deserve.

True believers of you are considered a fool

and naive as a dumb mule.

They may endure insult

and even be considered a cult.

In you there is much goodness and wisdom to show;

instead, people reap evil they sow.

Some accept part of what you say but not all;

it is why they err and fall.

You state your wisdom is better than gold;

sadly, billions miss this and are never told.

Nowadays, loathsome laws are made without your consent.

Again you are ignored; you they resent.

Mankind says, "We are greater than you;

concerning same-sex marriage, we have a better view."

When a nation calls wrong right and right wrong,

you teach it cannot stay strong.

You are not regarded as credible; you they resist.

Therefore, a nation will collapse and not exist.

Clerics and politicians profess to follow you and be wise,

but your true values they put aside and compromise.

You are thought of as not for real;

in the lives of people, no big deal.

To this world, you are something to ignore;

you are full of myths and a terrible bore.

Preferred over you are money, sports, entertainment, and drugs,

or a licentious lifestyle for many thieves and thugs.

Many think you are a faker

because you glorify a Maker.

Of you people believe what they wish to believe;

the rest they throw away and leave.

You stand for wisdom and purity

but are forsaken in the shadows of obscurity.

Your word reflects your Author's light,

which men hide from and even fight.

A believer of you could be in danger today;

his life could be destroyed and taken away.

You say a nation rejecting you falls under a curse;

I do not know of anything that could be worse.

Never has a book been so defamed and maligned;

people may study you, but the truth they never find.

Many wear a Christian masquerade,

carrying you to church, putting you on parade.

They profess of you to be a believer,

only to be a hypocritical deceiver.

To know and understand you they profess,

but your truths they do not confess.

The laws that you speak about are defied;

practicing and doing such works are denied.

Professing ministers, Bible, will take you in their hands and hold,

but preaching your truths, they are not bold.

If the world could abide by only one Bible rule,

it would be greatly improved and less cruel.

If everyone would think not to steal,

how good even an atheist would feel.

Your true seventh day and holy days' observance are forsaken;

for professing Christians, that is only Jewish, negated and mistaken.

You oppose days of Christmas, Easter, Halloween, or valentine,

stating they are of heathen source, or counterfeit Christian, not divine.

There is a devil you also speak about.

He deceives the world; his ministers say not, "Come out."

The Ten Commandments were removed from public, not to be seen;

what is viewed instead, lewd entertainment and things obscene.

For pleasures and cares of life the world is considerate;

unfortunately, to you, the world is Bible illiterate.

In the atheistic mind, we are as an insignificant fly;

we live for a short, purposeless time and forever die.

You speak of a creator God;

that for many is so odd.

A brainless, somehow thoughtful, organized bang

theory is more realistic;

your foolish designer idea is too simplistic.

What you say of eternal paradise

is only mythical and too nice.

There is news that is good,

though not understood.

Your prophecies of Christ's return

will be a time when people about you will learn.

Your promise the world will be at peace;

war, poverty, crime, and death will cease.

Instead of a world of getting, attitudes will change to giving,

outgoing concern, sharing; serving is what makes life worth living.

What will be lifted is a veil;

truth and righteousness will prevail.

To have you, Bible, in my possession and mind is a great pleasure;

you are more valuable than the sum of this world's treasure.

We are thankful for what the Eternal has written on your pages;

we understand redemption and life for eternal ages.

We can think about our change, a better resurrection,

some better thing;

this is the true hope and purpose to humanity you bring.

Bible, you are the greatest of all;

no other book stands as tall.

1

America, If I Were Your Enemy

America, if I were your enemy, I would flood your land with
illegal aliens as my first way to attack,
burdening you so much to break your financial back.
I would sell off farmland to foreigners to harvest their grains
and any fruit crop
to ship it out for themselves, leaving you not a drop.
Your taxes would be so much and high,
businessmen would run away from you and fly.
To make you a banana republic society
would be for me a great priority.
With processed foods of chemicals and fat, I would make
your heart and arteries clog,
giving you all you want as you stuff yourself and eat like a hog.
I would allow you access to all drugs, cigarettes you crave,
so cancer can kill you as you gasp and choke to your grave.
I would keep the illegal foreigners coming to plunder,
rape, and kill;
this would give your enemy a big thrill.
Instead of giving you real news, I would feed you with fluff,

distracting you with sports figures, entertainers, that kind of trivial stuff.

Your unborn babies, I would encourage you to kill through surgery or the morning-after pill.

2

America, If I Were Your Enemy

I would encourage certain criminals to appear sweet and
innocent by hiding behind the cruel race card lie
and have the guiltless defender to always look like the bad guy.
It would please me to see some people riot and loot
with an excuse to steal, burn, and even shoot.
To degenerate you more, I would encourage filthy lyrics
of rock and rap,
dulling you psychologically into a prolonged nap.
Judeo-Christian religious freedom and beliefs I would assault
and take away
to contribute to your corruption and moral decay.
I would make your armed forces so weak and thin,
in event of enemy attack,
you couldn't defend yourself to win.
You tried to buy peace with the Iranian nuclear deal.
You are guaranteed nothing; for them a big steal.
Reasoning with sharks, alligators, piranha, or a venomous snake
will prove to be a big mistake.
I would encourage you to reason with the incorrigible
and cruel

so you can play the world's biggest fool.

To give away such a large sum

is an example of your pathetic wis-dumb.

For Iranians to inspect Iranians is the proverbial fox

to guard the house of hens;

your naiveté and stupidity never ends.

If I were your enemy, America, you would make my task

to destroy you easy. I would just smile;

you are doing these things to yourself all the while.

Because of all your weighted corruption and vice,

I would wait for you to fall through thin ice.

The only thing for an enemy to do is finish you off with

a nuclear blasting;

your cities would be ashes and no longer would be lasting.

This would not give me any satisfaction or glory,

but for a real victorious enemy, it would be to him

a wonderful, thrilling story.

1

Even So, Come, Lord Jesus

Rev. 22:20

Come soon, Lord Jesus. The world desperately needs you here;

people are suffering in poverty, despair, hopelessness, and fear.

Wars, violence, evil, and corruption never cease;

you are the world's only salvation for the world peace.

Even your called elect suffer and groan

from the seeds of evil, humans have sown.

You, at first, will not be a welcomed sight,

for humanity will turn on you and even fight.

Because of you, the world shall wail;

nations rebel against you and wretchedly fail.

Humanity, being full of anger and blasphemy, will attempt to hide

as you execute your fierce wrath to break their stubborn pride.

Many deny that you are the creator, savior, and Christ existing;

for millennia, people denied and profaned you, your truths resisting.

You will be seen by every eye

when you descend from on high.

The spirit of antichrist has always prevailed;

more than ever are your true values being assailed.

There are people who profess to know you, so they think;

in evil works, perverse lifestyle, they make your name to stink.

Because the world is full of their religions and deities,

there is so much confusion;

they will not accept or recognize you because of so much delusion.

You stated that you are the way, truth, and life to see;

the world, at first, will not understand your teachings or agree.

As stated in Zechariah, on Mount Olives will you place your feet;

Satan and the world's government will you overthrow and defeat.

Then you will heal the blind, sick, lame, and the deaf will hear;

people will live in peace, having nothing to fear.

Your intervention, to put it mildly, will be rude;

nations will be overthrown and subdued.

In time, people will see you as king of kings

as you teach them peaceful and wonderful things.

With the world-ruling prophesied Prince of Peace,

poverty, suffering, and man's inhumanity to man will cease.

Even so, come, Lord Jesus, with your power and glory so strong.

Here you are sorely needed; here you belong.

1

Good Riddance to Satan

Known as the prince of the power of the air,

Satan works on human sentiments, causing depression and despair.

His character is of rage, jealously, gloom, and doom;

we must not in our lives give him any room.

His business is to shoot the fiery darts,

dividing humanity into many opposing parts.

He appears to be an angel of light,

but God and his people will he fight.

Prince of the world and darkness is for what he is known;

from him no truth or light is ever shown.

When we see deceit, dishonesty, cruelties, and terrorists strike,

we see his children reflecting and imitating what he is like.

Hatred, stealing, cheating, murdering, any detestable thing

is what Satan and his host of demons to this world bring.

Known also as the father of lies,

honesty and virtue are things he will despise.

Influencing people to hate beauty, truth, or anyone of goodness

is his way.

His desire is to cause suffering, grief, misery, war, even world

annihilation one day.

The good news is this will not happen; at Christ's return, he will
be bound;

his present misrule and influence on earth will not be around.

Satan will be out of human lives and gone;

the light of Christ on the world will one day dawn.

No longer troubles and strife will he instigate;

the world, under Christ, will be in a peaceful and happy state.

He will no longer be able to reign

with his mind, cruel and insane.

Since Satan's ministers will no longer exist,

his false teachings will not persist.

2

Good Riddance to Satan

Once called, Lucifer, having incredible gifts, the bringer of light,

became proud, lifted up; he turned on his Maker to overthrow and fight.

Ascending to heaven against God's government, he rebelled;

at the speed of lightning was he cast down and repelled.

Now he is called Satan, which means adversary;

his thinking, effect on the world, is to God contrary.

Being permitted to misrule for a while,

his influence will be cut off and out of style.

Troubles to the earth, for a while longer, he may send,

but he and his demons know they are losers at the end.

While Satan is mighty, we can in the meantime turn to the Almighty to pray;

scripture says that will cause him to flee and run away.

Good-Bye, America

Good-bye, America. Sorry to see you go,

seeing your character and morals have sunk so low.

Spiritually and morally, you are bankrupt;

your imaginations are utterly corrupt.

In the United States, the Bible is what many a person hates.

You are a land of persons without principle, not for real;

on the news, we watch how people steal.

Many see you as coming apart and dying,

and many of us are sighing.

Our freedoms we are losing

because of your own choosing.

You are a nation losing control of spending;

a disaster will be our ending.

It's been said we are on a financial *Titanic,*

and no doubt, we will be in a panic.

I see a gluttonous people who stuff themselves

and cannot control what they eat;

with stomachs in the way, they can't see their feet.

Sodom and Gomorrah is what Vladimir Putin called the United States;

interesting that a communist knows what God condemns and hates.

People are living together unmarried and in immorality

and even mock chastity and spirituality.

Life to unborn children is often denied.

The "thou shalt not kill" law is broken and defied.

Yet enough value is in the fetal tissue to be sold;

the attitude: "Get the money, go for the gold."

I look at this with appalling gravity,

an example of astonishing depravity.

Because of your undisciplined financial waste

and spending,

we see your debts building up with no ending.

With heavy taxes, ancient Rome declined.

You will not learn from them; you are blind.

You remind me of the symbolic Ezekiel harlot

who could not manage finances well;

filled with foolishness, she pays her clientele.

God bless America? Not anymore.

Illegal aliens rise above you; with you they wipe the floor.

Everybody from you wants more stuff;

you simply do not have enough.

You have the hit-and-run drivers who knock

people off their feet

as they speed callously down the street.

Today, you don't have real men in government

office with spine,

just spineless eunuchs buying votes to wine and dine.

Your people are full of profanities, expletives, and road rage;

unfortunately, that is the generation of this age.

To me it is a shame;

America, you're not the same.

Unlike other nations of the past,

your founding fathers gave you an incredible start.

You are less recognizable; Christian values force us to part.

No nation has been blessed as you in wealth, power, and prestige;

but now, America, your freedoms are under siege.

Sweet land of liberty? From every mountainside let freedom ring?

"Of thee," I find these words more difficult to sing.

You legalized same-sex marriages, calling it normal,

wonderful, and even cute;

people religiously opposed, you will prosecute and persecute.

As the betrayer, Judas, and with treasonous attack,

you brutally stabbed the US Constitution right in the back.

Freedom of religion and speech?

You're telling preachers what they can and cannot preach!

When Nigeria banned gay marriages, you threatened to cut off aid,

but with the bloody Castro boys, you are kissy face (and buttocks)

and anxious to trade.

In Jeremiah we read, "What wisdom is in them that reject God's word?" (Jer. 8:9).

To you this is revolting language, strange, not heard.

With your new laws, individual freedoms you interrupt;

will not the land, as the Bible stated, vomit you as you become more corrupt?

A number of people in a school were shot and killed;

with grief and sorrow, hearts were filled.

"Where was God?" someone asked, coming from a report.

"He wasn't there. You kicked him out. Remember?" came a retort.

You want God around only when things go wrong

but don't want Jesus' name mentioned in prayers, speech, or song.

You want his blessings and protection

but not his leadership and direction.

A moral compass you lack;

spiritually, you're off track.

I am much regretting

to see your sun setting.

What you lead the world in, without fail,

is having the most people in jail.

You cannot control your borders, spending, eating,

smoking, and alcohol;

sorry to say, the handwriting is on the wall for a fall.

Before the world, you apologize and cower;

you've lost the pride of your power.

In war time, you refuse to win;

sorry to say you are a "had been."

The world laughs and mocks at you in scorn

while you fill yourself with drugs and porn.

The only pride you have left is gay pride,

which you cherish at you side.

So corrupted are your processed foods with chemicals and junk

I wouldn't have the cruelty to feed them to animals, not even a skunk.

Criminals would be much more deserving,

as punishment from the foods you are serving.

A lot of your humor on television is sick and vile,

nothing to look at and smile.

Your unmelodious "music" is full of screaming, shrieking, and moaning, no class;

it's more tolerable to listen to a braying jackass.

In the movies, sex, violence, and occult are what your minds thrive,

another reason you're taking a dive.

To a people of a once great and proud land, judgment

upon you will fall

so that you will know there is a God above after all.

There is more I could add,

but why make things more sad?

America, you have cancer;

turning to God is your only healing answer.

I will end on a happy and positive note;

there is a time coming when no one will have to vote.

Jesus will be the leader of the earth; man will have no choice.

After a bitter lesson, America and the world will follow God's laws, live well, and rejoice.

1

Good-Bye, Bull

Good-bye to you, bull.

Sorry you cannot live your life to the full.

Unfortunately, you are forced to fight;

this repulses me and gives me no delight.

There is no excuse

to allow such animal abuse.

Before you are engaged,

you are wounded to make you enraged.

It incenses me to see you placed in a ring

so people can watch you get pierced with

weapons that cause you pain and sting.

As you charge at a cape, people shout with great fervor and enjoyment

at the expense of your pain and merciless torment.

For people to take pleasure of this cruel sport

has to be an audience of a perverse sort.

I wonder how happy people would feel

if their backs were stabbed with sharp steel,

and have blood out of them spurt

so they could feel pain and hurt.

Here are a few suggestions to make the fight fair,

which I am sure no matador would think and dare:

let matadors be wounded proportionally in the same way;

they would never agree to this; you wouldn't see such a day.

Let the blood from their backs pour out in a steady stream;

at the piercing of the lance, they would scream.

Have their backs be stuck with picks

and see if they can perform their cruel and skillful tricks.

Since the bull has no place to hide and go,

make it a really good and fair show.

Remove the barriers the matadors hide behind;

you will see a bunch of sadistic cowards scared out of mind.

2
Good-Bye, Bull

Matadors need assistance as usually shown;

have only one man fight you, bull, as you fight alone.

Sorry, bull, to see how people can be so perversely thrilled

to see you suffer, bleed, and by a sword get killed.

For those who think they are brave and filled with great nerve,

if you should ever gore them, that's something they well deserve.

When you lift men and toss them around,

until they finally hit the ground,

they tempt fate;

how does that make one great?

Good-bye again, bull. You are an awesome creature to look

at and hear snort;

I look forward to the day when you will not be the object of a

cruel and sadistic sport.

My sympathy and compassion for you is full.

To the reading audience, I am sincere; I give you no bull.

Good-Bye, Death and Grave

Good-bye to you, death, because the Bible says you will

lose your sting;

your conquest over humanity will no longer be your thing.

One day you will lose your victory, o, grave;

humanity will no longer be your slave.

In our temporary life, the day comes when we draw our last breath;

why I am so positive is that even you are temporary, death.

Grave, even you are a temporary place for people who deserve rest.

God has decreed it that way; He knows what is best.

Grave and death, you will be a thing of the past

when the righteous are resurrected to glory so fast.

In a sense, your turn will come to die;

no longer will the sorrowful stand over you and cry.

Death and grave, you will be lost and forgotten,

something left behind;

no thought of you will ever again enter a spirit mind.

Both of you will have lost your power;

we, the victors, will over you tower.

Life to many is precious and dear;

the thought of you can install fear.

People will one day at their grave arrive,

but the righteous are destined to paradise, more than survive.

Death and grave, you are not the final end;

this is the message of hope to others I send.

(I Cor. 15)

1

Good Riddance, Cigarette

You are a scourge to the world, cigarette;

as popular as you are, you cause people much regret.

As people light you up and puff,

you fill them with your poisonous stuff.

You are small and wrapped up round,

but you have put many underground.

On you people get very stuck

because of smoke from you they suck.

For many you are their master, god, and idol,

causing many to become slowly suicidal.

People cannot seem to get enough of you;

you are with them always until their lives are through.

Money spent on you can be a big financial loss;

you are truly a very demanding boss.

Cigarette, you are something many people have married;

with health and money loss, you are a heavy cross to be carried.

When smokers afflicted with cancer die,

cigarette makers do not care or cry.

They would not for the smokers shed a tear;

loading up their bank accounts is important and dear.

They wouldn't send a flower or a lily;

that would be ridiculous, too silly.

Not even a sympathy card for relatives or a business thanks

concerning the deceased sucker who sent them smiling to their banks.

Cigarette, you are worthless, destructive, and you throw

off an offensive smell;

your toxic smoke can harm and destroy children and

nonsmokers as well.

Your obnoxious smoke drifts to me at a stoplight or

even a beach.

You are hard to get away from; you have so much reach.

Sadly, the marijuana and tobacco weed

appeal to the selfish and false sensual need.

2

Good Riddance, Cigarette

To me you are the devil's tool,

turning a smart person into a self-destroying fool.

If every smoker gave up on you and quit,

the air would be cleaner, people would be healthier

and fit.

As for medical costs, there would be less spending.

Your days in the millennium will be over, a time

for your ending.

That includes your costars: chewing tobacco, pipes,

"drugs," and cigars.

Good riddance to you, cigarette;

when you're gone, you will be undesirable, people happier

and without regret.

Good-Bye, Good Credit Score

Good-bye, good credit score.

The loss of you made many financially sore.

Hope some day you will return,

something for which many yearn.

The housing market came to a burst

when the unscrupulous, never satisfied, put themselves first.

Because of the theft and cruelty of inflation,

there was, for people, no consideration.

As expenses increased and became too high,

many had to say to their homes, "Good-Bye."

People had to live in a car or a tent;

they couldn't pay the mortgage or rent.

Because of such covetousness and insatiable money lust,

then came the inevitable housing bubble bust.

Hopefully, this is a lesson and experience for humanity,

not to get ourselves overly concerned about the money vanity.

Hope you do come back, good credit score;

how we would welcome many or just a few points more.

1

Good-Bye, Money

All of us will have to say "Good-Bye", to you, money,

even though to people you are as honey.

People can put you to a lot of good use

but often wastefully and with much abuse.

Biblically, the love of you is the basic evil root,

producing works of very bad fruit.

For you, people lie, kill, bribe, war, and steal;

it tells us how much about you people feel.

Of you, people want more and more;

never satisfied, you are what they adore.

The lack of you can cause worry and stress,

concerning bills, food, and clothes for dress.

People find you so hard to come by,

causing many to despair and sigh.

Not many years after one's birth,

many struggle to draw you out of a reluctant earth.

Proverbs state you have wings that can fly away

after acquiring riches or even a day's pay.

Bank accounts can for a while grow.

A time comes to leave them; when, we never know.

People can work for you and become very aggressive.

They will work so hard and long; you are that impressive.

For many you may be a great obsession;

in a sense, they become your possession.

Jesus stated, "Man's life consists not in things he possesses,"

but for you, money, man obsesses.

Money, there is nothing with you that is wrong;

man's priorities and misuse places you where you don't belong.

You can be wasted in the hands of a fool

or used wisely as a giving, helpful, and purposeful tool.

You have limits; happiness, peace of mind, good health

you do not guarantee.

Many understanding this would have to agree.

You cannot stop aging, death, or pain;

pursuing you can be so vain.

Even after we accumulate and do much to achieve,

you, money, we shortly have to leave.

Concerning our appointment to the grave,

you cannot intervene for us and save.

Scripture states: "Set your affections above, not on earth";

wisdom, true values, eternal life, and purpose are far more

than you are worth.

Treasures up in heaven we are told to lay

so that we can attain eternal life one day.

Money, you cannot be used to bribe or buy one's way in God's

kingdom for any amount;

access comes only through faith, grace, and righteous character.

That is what really and truly will count.

Good-Bye, World

Good-bye, world. You are, without doubt,
on your way out.
You are setting up your stage
as we head for a new age.
If I were to die now, your system I would never miss;
I would be in peace and sweet bliss.
I would not be leaving paradise;
your ways are treacherous, full of vice.
From your beginning, there has been war, hunger,
and strife,
resulting in suffering and horrible loss of life.
Everywhere I look and hear from news around,
evil in you does continually abound.
We hear about theft, violence, scandal, and rape;
this kind of news is hard to escape.
Your financial pressures cause many to be stressed;
how much from this do we need peace and rest.
You go after one's income with a sharp, heavy ax;
you chop away, cut, and brutally tax.
When people are blessed with an inheritance or a
good monetary gift deal,
you think you're entitled to something,

so you take and steal.

There is a view tax concerning even what people see,

another scheming way to collect government fee.

I see the theft of inflation and greed;

with big markups, people get far more than they need.

People have to work so hard and long

because of this pressure and wrong.

Under the guise of religion, you have people

whose life's mission is to kill,

glorifying and delighting in how much blood

they spill.

You are full of deception and lies;

the good and truthful, you may kill and despise.

You always had cruel tyrants in existence,

putting people through horrific experiences without resistance.

You never improved; with such history of blood and gore,

you now have weapons to kill more efficiently than ever before.

Your weapons of mass destruction can destroy nations

off the earth's face,

potentially destroying every member of the human race.

"Peace, peace," you cry.

You never mean it; how you lie.

Thankfully, there's a day when the Prince of Peace will come

to save the world from destruction and these evils from.

When he appears, your tribes will mourn;

they will wish they were never born.

They will be filled with anger and disdain;

Jesus will send them deadly plagues and pain.

There is hope because your deceiver and adversary, Satan,

will one day be removed;

how greatly, then, will the world be improved.

It will be like day and night;

nations will be honest and no longer fight.

The blind will see; the deaf will hear.

Jesus will be present, no need to fear.

You will see how people of infirmities heal;

world, you are in for a better and fantastic deal.

After some time, you will become converted and new,

something believed and understood by only a select few.

War, injustices, poverty, and cruelties will end;

this prophetic message to you I send.

You will be habitable, decent, uplifting,

a place one can call "nice";

you are destined to become a God-given paradise.

Good-Bye, Rusty

Good-bye, Rusty. To me and others, you were a great friend.

Sorry to see you fail and your life come to an end.

You were my companion when I was alone.

Happy and content were you, just to have a bone.

Because of your good shepherd looks, many heads turned;

your good-natured friendliness is what people about you learned.

Also, you were so alert and on guard,

barking at any stranger near the yard.

When I returned from work each day,

you were happy to see me and full of play.

So content were you, and full of fun

as you swam in the lake under the summer sun.

From your puppy days, I watched how you had grown;

I was proud to have you as my own.

With your beautiful coat of rust-like tan,

people marveled at the way you walked or ran.

Over a fence you would jump and clear

as the graceful leap of a deer.

Among mail carriers, you befriended

and followed them until delivery ended.

Mail customers would give you water or a doggy treat

to quench your thirst and give you something to eat.

You enjoyed the jogging, walking and a good car ride; wherever I went, you were often at my side.

Never complaining, deceitful, or harmful, Rusty,

you were better than some people, a friend so trusty.

As years passed, the aging process caused you to slow;

eventually, the time came when you had to go.

Thanks for the happy memories you left behind;

a dog truly can be the best friend a man can find.

Good Riddance, Sorrow, Disappointment, and Pain

Good riddance to, you, sorrow, disappointment, and pain;

you will be gone during Christ's millennial reign.

You, sorrow, which have brought people depression and sadness,

will be replaced with contentment and gladness.

You have brought regret to people, disappointment,

but will be replaced by God's healing anointment.

Isaiah 35:10 states that sorrow and sighing shall flee away;

the world and God's people ache and groan for that day.

One may ask, "Why has God, if there be a God, allowed you to exist for so long?"

Answer: Since the fall of Adam, God is proving, for a while, that man's ways are wrong.

The good news is that the world will have a positive change and a new start;

Jesus will be sent to heal the sick, blind, infirm, and broken of heart (Isa. 61:1, Luke 4:18).

The earth will be filled with the knowledge of the Lord as the waters cover the sea (Isaiah 11:9).

People will learn and comply with God's law and, after a time, happily with him agree.

Sometimes circumstances of life or people can throw us a cruel curve.

We may feel we suffer wrongfully for something we do not deserve.

In time of false accusation, friend or spouse betrayal, a fiery trial not understood,

just think about Jesus who went about doing good (Acts 10:38).

Instead of being appreciated, he was severely scourged and to a cross cruelly nailed

to redeem a thankless, wicked, depraved world that has miserably and spiritually failed.

The time will come when Christ's elect will be gathered with him forever (1 Thess. 4:17).

When will we see you again, sorrow, disappointment, and pain? The answer is never!

Good-Bye, Poems

I must now say good-bye to each poem.

I was happy to write and have you in my home.

The time has come for the poem writing to end

so that certain messages we can get out and send.

The opportunity to write

can be to the writer and reader a delight.

Certain ideas poem writers are expressing

can be entertaining, insightful, or impressing.

The thoughts and writing action

can give reader and writer satisfaction.

It can be both work and fun

as poem writings are being done.

Certain things written in you

will be, to some, unfamiliar and new.

Not everyone will understand and agree,

but some will; just wait and see.

Good-bye again, poems. Somewhere along the line,

the discerning ones will think you are fine.

Printed in the United States
By Bookmasters